MW00879097

This Dewdrop World

OTHER BOOKS BY JAMES JUST

A Year of Days

Sketches of Poás

Meanders

The Book of Noah

This Dewdrop World

by

James Just

Cover design and illustration: Gesa Emde
Waldsee, etching
www.gesaemde.de

Published by Poás Press

First Edition

Table of Contents

This Dewdrop World

For She

I have always been drawn
by windblown clouds
into dreams of a lifetime
of wandering.

— Matsuo Bashō, from
Narrow Road to the Interior

Watercolors

Best part of a year spent
wrestling to write
each day a struggle
to sit at the desk
mind at wander
legs, fingers
itching to stretch.

Henry Miller
when words wouldn't flow
would swap pen for brush
words for pigments
let images stream
from eyes of a child
to scamper and laugh
across paper fields
spirit refreshed
with watercolors.

Beyond the screen
outside the window
a lush hillside beckons
gloved hands, shovel
shears, Japanese hoe
to sculpt a landscape.

A garden begins
to slowly take form
dappled in hues
of leaf and flower.

I liked it better back then

I liked it better back then
Marycruz says.

Our vet and I
drive to Heredia
Bela the black lab
sitting in the back
right knee blown out.
Afternoon, rush hour
a general strike
in protest of new taxes
intersections blockaded
the autopista too
Marycruz minding Waze
winding back roads
those too jammed
a one-hour trip
crawling to three
light turning night.
I'm lost, she says
no idea where we are
she went here to vet school
ten years ago, maybe
still looks so young.

Curving down in the dark
a road smoothly paved
cement sidewalks fronting
new houses behind walls
we stop at barrier arms.
The university, rear entrance
we came in the back way
didn't recognize a thing.
She pauses a moment.

4

I used to walk here, road dirt
hills covered in coffee
shaded by trees.

A guard walks to her window
cell phones permission
then raises the gate
parking lot, empty
the clinic, dark.
Marycruz buzzes the door
a few moments, it opens
hackles raised, Bela growls
at an intern in green scrubs
masked, too, in green
against COVID-19.
We enter the lobby
disinfect feet and hands
the intern, Marycruz
Bela on leash
disappear down a hallway.

Your appointment, you're late
the surgeon gruffs
I'm ready to go home
you'll have to come back.
(Marycruz tells me this later
returning to Grecia
relating the scene.)
I was so stressed
the drive, horrific
in a wreck, almost
to all be for nothing
Bela to suffer
days more on drugs.

The surgeon, softened

rolls Bela in a sling
hefts her up, lays her out
x-rays of game leg
displaying the damage
surgery scheduled
for next afternoon.

Bela settled in kennel
the surgeon asks
to be dropped off downtown
we then head back home
pass front of the college
street broad, bordered
with business and high-rise.
A girlfriend and I,
we used to walk here
along the old road
narrow, winding
through fields of coffee
Marycruz says.
We'd each carry a big stick
to beat off any man
should jump out of the bushes.
Finger taps her iPhone
clipped to the dash
music turned off
the car falls quiet.

I liked it better back then.

December, slopes of the volcán

winds trade in clouds
Poás enshrouded
arroyo alight
arced in colors

The boys in the band

January, daybreak
awakened from sleep
by rapping on glass
a clay-colored thrush
at the slider, his pecks
punctuated by high hops
wings beating the pane.

Jump out of bed
chase him away
but quick, he's back.
Dawn follows dawn
ears muffled in pillows
the mind drifts . . .

Back on the farm
fast asleep in the loft
jolted awake
tin roof booming
*rat-a-tat-**tat**-tat*
*rat-a-**tat tat tat**.*
Stumble naked down stairs
throw open the front door
to a crisp spring morning
at the corner of sheep shed
serves as our home
a red-breasted sapsucker
hammers the gutter drain
bill tip a bead
metal pipe, a drum
gutters, tin roof resounding.
Peppered with pebbles
the bird takes flight.

8

The drumming repeats
daybreaks that follow
stretching the week.
"I'll teach him," strapping
a length of downspout
to trunk of a near oak
"to hammer at this tree
not be scrammed off."

Next day dawning
sucker's back on stage
I run buck to my pipe drum
wielding a screwdriver
shank, the stick
handle, the mallet
reprise the bird's rhythm
*rat-a-tat-**tat**-tat*
*rat-a-**tat tat tat***
the bird throws me a look
we take turns rapping strophic.

Curtain rises with sun
morn following morn
bird clinging his corner
we tapping our beat.
One session a pheasant
pops out of the pasture
wings whirring, belts out
*"c-c-**cauu** ca"*
drops back in tall grass
then pops up again
*"c-c-**cauu** ca."*
A wild turkey in turn
hops up on a stump

puffs out his chest
rustles his wings
stretches his neck
*"**gobl**goblgoblgobl"*
repeating the ritual
sings out once more
*"**gobl**goblgoblgobl."*

Ruckus of thrush
recalls to the present
and the germ of a poem
long dormant unfolds
begins to take form

Cool dawn aroused
vaunting their plumage
in dance and song
the boys in the band.

Reply to an email from a friend

"the sun has become disgusted with waiting"

Rick I was thinking
the poem you sent me
— *Finish* —
was something of yours
until I reached
the very last line
    — Bukowski

Nothing

morning clear
frolic of breeze
our two dogs race
the track to the road

to do

trees wave and rustle
skin tingles at sun's touch
moist dog noses snuff
detritus aside asphalt

to do

top of the drive
neighbors smile good day
dogs scout about
for a while, return

nothing

A walk to the waterfall

In the morning we're going
to walk to the waterfall
Irina says
Marilyn, Paul, Shamroe
we've never found the way
Ligia will guide us
why don't you come along?
Perhaps the hike
will inspire a new poem,"
sweetening the offer.

Consider a moment
the trek unfolding
girls together, in front
bubbling chatter
Paul, Shamroe buddied up
talking whatever
guys talk about
myself, off
somewhere else.

Thanks, I'll stay here
Joe should be coming
to patch up the portico
Isaac will be here
at work in the garden
Diego might show
to fix the clothes dryer
Marlene, it's her morning
to clean the house.
You all go along
have a good time.

'Bye Baby, she says

from the driveway, leaving
to join up with the others.
Joe had texted
he wouldn't be coming.
Isaac switched days.
Diego called, saying
he'd be here next week.
Marlene, she's here
will need a ride home
up the hill when she's done.

The casita, the computer
screen a blank page
in the loft, the kitty
awakes from her nap
slips from her pouf
clomps down the stairs
hops onto the desk.
Cool nose touches mine
asking that her fur
thick, long, and fine
be brushed and plucked
of burr and bramble.
She flops on the desk
purring, twists and turns
from side to side
the while flicking her tail
licking her paws
washing her ears.
Primping complete
she curls to a comma
corner of the desktop
a paw over face
her eyelids drop.

Marlene near done

rise from the swivel chair
kitty quick stakes her claim.

La vacuna (the vaccination)

Be here tomorrow
one o'clock, the voice said
Irina answering the phone
deciphering the Spanish
your husband too
list starting with oldest
now having reached us.

Next day drive
to the local clinic
four klicks down the hill.
A burly guard uniformed
brown and black at the gate
gathers IDs
stacks them on a table
mouths a muffled
go wash your hands
finger pointing
to sink at the back.

Old folks sit patient
chairs two meters apart
outside, under cover
chatting with neighbors
eyes alight above masks
ladies well put together
clothes cloaking their bodies
in complementary colors
men weathered, withered
wear trousers, sport shirts
less carefully chosen.

A door opens, Elsa
who rules at reception

largesse straining
the top of her scrubs
crosses the lobby
grabs the stack of IDs
turns about, retreats
flashes Irina a smile
her good will won
with chocolate chip cookies.

The minutes pass
so too young women
stride the spaced crowd
to dates with their doctors
bearing their babies
in arms, in bellies
unlike their elders
scant coverage, the clothes
clinging their contours.

Elsa at intervals
calls by name
and one by one
the summoned slowly
walk, or shuffle
with aid of an arm
disappear through the door
finally a turn mine.

Down a hall to the left
a nurse trim in white sits
at a desk stacked with records.
I take a chair set beside
we banter a few moments.
Another nurse behind mask
appearing twin of the first
raises my sleeve

cold cottons my shoulder
plunges a needle
plasters the puncture.
The first returns my ID
folded in cardstock
carné de vacunación
noting date of first dose
and that for the second
in exactly three weeks
same time, same station.

Inoculants are asked
to wait in reception
for fifteen minutes
to ensure no reaction
but rains coming early
thunder hurling fat drops
and lacking umbrellas
we rush to the car
outracing the deluge.

That same afternoon
a call alerts Rick
his appointment, next day.
I'm so happy, he says after
I'm no longer afraid,
I'm not going to die.

I don't dig that well anymore

I don't dig that well anymore
Jane explains
asking for help
rearranging the little patch
of garden between porch
and concrete pad carport
movie the *pincel*
to border the drive side
grub out the grass
turn over the earth
set new plants to curtain
her purview of car.
Could you help, bring Isaac?

Saturday morning early
show with shovel and rake
selection of plants gleaned
from gardens of friends
and three sacks of compost
from Lili's nursery up the road.
Work done before lunch
soil turned, plants set
to grow in light loam.

I'm so happy! Jane says
email the next morning.
I love to garden but
I've been a bit down.
Your hand, so heartening.
I'm very grateful.
Thanks to Isaac, and you
generosity of friends
I don't dig
that well anymore.

On hearing from my sister

I heard from Peggy
my sister remaining
near where we were born
north of Sacramento

railing

of heat, of smoke
fires in the foothills

ranting

of lakes and rivers
shrunken to mud
trickle of faucet
reduced to drips
while around her, rolling
through vast fields of farms
long rows of wheeled sprinklers
spurt out great streams.
I'm so angry, she said
greed, blindness, inertia.
My coming to see
is so shocking to me.
All of these years
I've been Pollyanna.

Within me her furor
ferments for days
then one night, a dream.

We're sitting at a table
sheltered patio outdoors
a restaurant, Midtown

near to the one, young
she worked for me once.

I lean in, speak softly.
"Remember those days?
People lined at the door
money rolling in, thinking
to always be more
but in truth, fated
to pull down the pillars
damned with shame
those left in the rubble.

"That day we talked
concerning your future
'Get out!' I gritted
'Get out while you can.'"

Distance, and time
the end approaching
such drama now seeming
so small, so human.

An email to my daughter

The other day I saw
a catchy climate change graphic
posted on Facebook
by my daughter, a teacher
a comic strip titled
"Climate Change, a Timeline."

A bar graph, four segments
the first, taking up
about half the length
colored turquoise, ballooned
"Climate change isn't real."
The second, in orange,
around forty percent
concedes "Okay it's real,
but we're not convinced
it's caused by humans."
Three-quarters of the remaining
bright red, blurting "Oops."
The last tiny bit
a sick yellow, "Fuck."

The post prompted me
to write her an email.

Hi Shana, Irina showed me
your post on Facebook
bringing to mind loss
of something, of someone
beloved, the grieving.

Most of our friends here
well-read, enlightened
don't seem to fathom

22

the calamity, tragedy
centuries in the making
beginning now to hit home.
Or perhaps, they do see
talk, just hot air.

Your strip, ending
something, I think, missing.

Remember watching the movie
The Treasure of the Sierra Madre
at the end, tall the gold dust
gleaned at such pain
from those wild mother mountains
strewn to the wind
and Howard — Walter Huston —
begins to laugh
deep, from the belly
Curtain — Tim Holt —
a moment, joins in
both going then their ways
getting on with living.

I dream that someday
we share such laughter.

Love, Dad

Choices

I had a good friend
who once casually said
I believe we become
the fruit of our choices.

One day, wobbly
she went to a doctor
sent to a hospital
an array of tests
a tumor, glioma
top of her brainstem.

Weeks, a handful
to become vegetable
another, of days
to become dead.

Passionfruit caterpillars

On the patio tiles
a writhing black lump
caterpillars, traveling faster
than any single one
could crawl, alone.

The larval mass, rolling
those on the ground crawling
at normal speed
those climbing their backs
cover twice the distance
those running on top
nearly four times as fast
all swapping positions
each taking their turn.

So report studies
theory, math, measure.
But often, watching
them out in the open
without seeming aim
ambling for hours
then at rest, roiling
dark bodies soaking
warmth of sun.

This morning the mass
quickly crossing ceramic
disappears into dense
green growth of garden.

Giant spiny walking stick

At break of dawn
a twelve-inch stick
clings to the screen
of the bedroom slider.

Phasmids feed in the night
rest during the day
disguise of twig
to keep predators away.

This one, three legs
but, little mind
walking sticks regrow
parts left behind.

Female, most surely
they don't need to copulate
hatchlings same-sexed
why breed a mate?

The stick later walking
off with the light.

Some days

Some days, restless
hands and feet yearn
to get away from the desk
the sitting, thinking

whole morning work
hacking heliconias
to make way for new growth
green shoots, bright blooms

drag the detritus
down to the brush pile
toss onto to the top
to slowly compost

under the overgrowth
plants shaded, strangled
freed, to find
their place in the sun

boots grow heavy
jeans stain with mud
shirt soaks in sweat
time to quit, to lunch

afterwards, beat
a path to the sofa
rest after noon
not quite asleep

What do you say
to a son to whom
you've never been father?

*"I read what you wrote
on your Facebook page
health, vision fading.
I'm so sorry."*

Words
so hollow
so little
so late.

*"I love you.
Dad."*

Perspectives, Guatemala

I. Chiapas, Mexico: an accident

A highway, a curve
a truck, fully loaded
tips over, slides into
a concrete abutment

the container carried
splits open spilling people
sardined inside, about
one hundred sixty-five

though who can be sure
witnesses say
some ran away
including the driver

fifty-five dead
one hundred six, hospitaled
men, women, children
mostly *guatemaltecos*

on their way to the U.S. of A.
more than anything reaching out
for the American dream
says a survivor, just a kid
back home, no future
can't get ahead

expressing sadness
for the dead, the injured
U.S. ambassador twitters
please don't risk your lives
policy being that

migrants not come.

II. Guatemala: sightseeing

A good friend of mine
an expat, Costa Rica
writes he's inspired
to travel Latin America

posting on his blog
notes of his travels
with plenty of photos
places, birds, people

from Lake Atitlán
flanked by volcanos
around its shores, scattered
twelve smallish pueblos

those vying for tourists
display vibrant color
restaurants, street vendors
charming hotels

culture, dress Mayan
the people, get around
foot, tuk-tuks or *lanchas*
criss-crossing the waters

take chicken bus to Antigua
streets cobble, style Spanish
people there, too
awash in bright hues

so picturesque, visitors
in jeans and sneakers

tee-shirts, brash tops
grab sights with their iPhones

affordable, friendly
jawdroppingly beautiful
my friend avows
many places to yet go
no time for repeat visits
but I'll find the time
to get back to Antigua.

Sunday, before the new year

mid-morning, clouds
driven by trades
enshroud the volcán
softly, mist falls

chases a poet
from mindless pleasure
of soil, of sweat
of solitude

to retreat inside
sit at the desk
the void, the promise
of a raw page

Conspiracy

There are theories afloat
posing global elites
conspire to cull
the world's population
various means including
disease, drugs, vaccines.

A notion far-fetched
to one unsung
far removed from high circles
to enlist such conspiracy
might prove imprudent
as plans oft go awry
and history cautions
that in times of turmoil
the rich risk their heads.

Consider a moment
what need to conspire?
future unfolding
as it will and must
people borning, dying
as conditions provide
humans but one species
among countless others
exploiting, excreting
evolving, extincting.

Gaia patient, indifferent
her time too fleeting
as the universe itself.

Letter to a friend in the States

Nothing much going on
staying close to home
COVID raging
as never before

work around the house
steel rusted needs repaired
or replaced, scraped, painted
getting ready for rain

life feels to be flying
one season ending
turn right around
to come once again

remember, as a child
the week, stretching
end forever in coming
to be freed from school

haven't written much lately
seems never the time
and when time is
nothing keeps coming

car back from the shop
the day spent running
bank, groceries, dentist
wisdom teeth need pulled

sorry the short note
got to move sprinklers
the garden, thirsty
stay in touch, pura vida.

Full moon

Dawn, the moon rests
ripe on the ridge

day to be spent
getting ready for rains
soon to arrive clock-like
one full moon, two new

thirteen cycles to a year
a full life, a thousand
to me left allotted
a hundred more, maybe.

Neighbor, above
felled some of his pines
and with, down came dirt
buried ditch along drive

to me falls the task
of clearing the drainage
twenty shovels to a wheelbarrow
twenty loads, two hours

these days, a day's work
flagging now more quickly
than in time past
take lunch, then nap

job stretches the week
while men work on the roof
and gutters, rotted
bitter breath of Poás

should finish up today

noon after full moon.

Interregnum

One morning mid-March
the trades hold their breath

the sky clear
blue
heat
heightens with sun

clouds after noon
gather
glower
shower the evening

soil dry, pale
moistens
softens
darkens enticing

leaves quiescent
swell
stretch
sparkle in moonlight

new day, yigüirro
dares one lilting strain

Trash; or, the wise man of dream

Our land reaches up to
and along the main road
shoulder graded, sloped
to channel a deluge

Appears there one morning
a huge heap of rubbish
sharded with shatter
ranging the frontage.

Couple days later
the mountain has moved
litter lavished in stead
foam, rubber, plastic
glass and metal
bits and chunks
left tangled in tall grass.

The whole of a morning
stooped under sun
gloved hands pluck
and stuff detritus
into sturdy feed sacks.

Baking in heat
sweating, swearing
three bags clean full
trussed and tossed
in back of the Sidekick
hauled to the trash bin.

Such gatherings of garbage
appearing recurrent
three, four times a year

38

a few days before pickup
trash suddenly mounts
reaching head high
stretching the road
a good measure of meters.

I stew to myself
once again cleaning up
how people can think
to toss their trash
onto land of a stranger
not asking permission
leaving to another
a big mess behind.

One night, a day dream
a neighbor, an old man
neatly dressed, clean shaven
sits on his porch
as I walk by
hot, dirty, angry
"Buenas," he says
and I in reply.
"You seem out of sorts
this morning, my friend."
"It's the trash," I reply
"Bad enough it's dumped
on my property, worse
the scraps left behind
to be dealt with myself.
I've been thinking, a sign
'No botar basura'"
no dumping trash here.

The old man, silent
rubs his chin, ponders

for a moment, then speaks.
"Your land, your ditch
don't you cut back the brush
keep clear the drainage?"
"I do," I acknowledge
with nod of head.
"Why don't you," he offers,
"cut the grass just before
then rake up the leavings
the cleanup then easy."
I fix his eyes, dumbed.
"Adiós," he says
getting up, going in.

The months pass
garbage hauls, too
people setting out trash
sprinkled with treasures
for neighbors to glean.
One day after pickup
I grab my gloves
a rake, and sacks
set out to clean up
when across the street
the man whose business
makes most of this mess
sees me, stops
steps out of his truck
crosses the road
and, without speaking
begins to bag
what I rake into piles
fifteen minutes, we're done.

"Muchas gracias," I say
"A usted," he replies

thank *you* very much
we shake hands in parting
and I say, in silence
to the wise man of dream
Muchas gracias, adiós.

Ravished

an orchid blossom
in its purple resplendent
leafhopper ravished

Freshening

One morning awaken
the *I* that has been
many years passing
no longer is

breathe, deeply
the mind let go
empty, serene
that to unfold

days follow, early
don jeans, boots, gloves
step out to the land
crisp air of morning

shovel paths, lay beds
set plants in vision
of form, foliage, flower
prune, groom, watch

afternoon downpours
hammer the earth
slash slopes left bare
of green armor

keenly follow
how new plantings fare
watch if they flourish
in their new environs

here or there note
discord emergent
reweave the score
over, again

with time, measures
form composition
garden weaved
in harmony

years to come
the work to fade
as all of existence
dissolve but a dream

for a moment a man
grown wearied of will
freshened by hand
soil, sun, rain.

Requiem: Daria Dugina

A woman, so young
blown to bits in a car bomb
mothers, fathers, weep

Mac's dream

unbegotten

essence

a spark, primal

long ere

(mind unmoored
space, time, left behind)

species

all but a blip

vanished

nothing

forgotten

Waxing gibbous, the lune

Moon waxing gibbous
in the night sky
coyotes yip, yelp, cavort
the dogs bark, for once
don't charge the door
demanding let out.

Awoken from dream
wonder
what?
do they mean?

Dreams appear
absent of effort
painstakingly sketch
scenes seamlessly shift
recklessly race
through improv'd plots.

The mind, unminded
senseless of sense
clever, capricious
spewer of image
spinner of stories
at once forgotten.

One morning, plunged
into a laundry room sink
not deigning to drain
regardless of snake
or other tricks
of plumbing trade
mere droplets of water
wet soil beneath floor

seen, not to be reached
through crack in concrete.

That night, in sleep
mind ponders the problem
awaken with fix
precisely pictured.
Morning, set to the task
drain soon cleared
water sluiced
to flow where it ought.

At dinner, with friends
conversation touches
two wars, raging
other side of the globe.
Can't think about it
Paul says
it's just too horrible.

Mid night, drifting
hear the words echo
those people, not human
living on land
that, by God
is given to us
they must be wiped out
that there be peace.

Immersed in dream
unconscious, collective
themes, archaic
waxing gibbous, the lune.

This dewdrop world
— *Issa*

This world a dewdrop
nothing but a dewdrop world
and yet, and yet —

Dancing to the end of time

the moon, circling
always, just a bit
more quickly than the sun

at times ahead, racing
at times, chasing
round, round the heavens

ducking in
and out
of shadow

the movements, formal
dancing
to the end of time

¡Viva Viva!

Leaving, an errand
on the drive, our cat
lying there, still
stop the car, call out
her name, Viva
she meows, barely
raising her head.
Scrape her up, both hands
lay her down gently
back seat of the car
fly off to the vet.

She's so cold
Marycruz says
a few more minutes
she would have been dead
wrapping her in a heating pad
giving injections
for pain, infection.
She'll need to stay
watched a few days.

Marycruz calls the next week
Viva's ready to come home.
We run, pick her up.
An entry wound in her neck
right at the spine
Marycruz points
I found this at her throat
right under the skin
holds up a lead pellet
ziplocked in clear plastic.

A month later Viva

is up and around
though with manifest limp
of leftside legs
her once fluid leap
from floor to tabletop
where her food is set
to keep from the dogs
now staged with chair.

Afternoons Viva lies
on my desk on a pillow
purring when stroked
combed of debris
tangled in thick fur.
Comes and goes as pleases
at twilight, sky clear
garden steps warmed
by rays of the day
lies still, watching
the setting of sun.

Where are the birds?

where are the birds?
the day quiet
sky empty
of green flights of parakeets
frolicking chatter
of blue of parrots
shrieking in flocks
of swifts, swallows
diving, twisting

a yigüirro in a tree
sings softly to himself

normal, otherwise
temperatures, rain
unlike reports
from around the globe
of earth, cracked
heat, drought
scorched crops, forests
of storms, floods
sweeping all away

this year, when
the rains began
fall of night not feted
with flashing of fireflies
even the butterflies
failed to bloom
a bare handful
flit the lantana

a single hummingbird
haunts rabo del gato

sips flower to flower

high in the sky
a lone vulture scours
sole company, clouds

Blessed insignificance

the rains this season
late in arriving
earth darkens with moisture
hills deepen their green

the world far away
bloodied of bodies
ravaged by death
rattles of empire

here, a land blessed
left mostly alone
a people patient
reigning, peace

the girls walk Sundays
Marilyn's car quits
at the top of our road
sits there two days

this dawn it's gone
José has taken it
down to his shop
to be resurrected

a banana flowers red
orchids flaunt their colors
a thrush lilts his song
 the quiet of morning

Reflections on Robert Frost's
The Road Not Taken
in light of yet more war

Two roads diverged in a wood, and I—
I took the one less traveled by,
And that has made all the difference.

I. The text

The poem's *I* reminiscing
years ago, a wood, walking
at a fork, pauses
one path disappearing
behind brush at a bend

the *I* takes the other
less traveled, conceding
both worn about same
yellow leaves fresh fallen
unbruised, untrodden

thinking, leave the first
perhaps another day
noting, perforce
how way leads to way
discounting return

concluding, the *I*
in hindsight sees prescience
the key to providence
to be telling his tale
years to yet come.

That poem, a tricky one
Frost would say

read, the text, closely.

II. The context

England, a village, 1915
there Robert Frost
and kindred poets
one, Edward Thomas,
Robert's companion
ramble the countryside
Thomas choosing a road
later lamenting
not taking the other.

The poem, penned playful
Frost later explained
having sent it to Thomas
who failing to see fun
took it rather to heart
been goaded, enlisted
before long to be dead
shot clean through the chest
the battle of Arras.

I'm never so serious
Frost later would quip
as when I'm joking.

Sometimes at night

Sometimes at night
depths of darkness
relentless in dream
vivid, reviewing
foibles of youth
failures to follow
abruptly, awake
steeped in shame.

Sit up, breathe
rise, step outside
the moon, waxing
sky sparkling stars
hills silent, serene.
A few moments, return
dogs fast asleep
Bela, her sheepskin
Capo, his bed

to mine I return
spirit now settled
slip under the covers
mindful not to disturb
she by my side
who, even so, loves me.

A glance of an eye

A four-lane road
hemmed commercial
autos stream both ways
two young men on motos
rush an ebb in the flow
roaring, racing
the youth on the left
peeks right at his rival

from a parking lot out
zips a white compact
threads oncoming traffic
slips into a slot
in front of the cycle
the youth, distracted
brakes late, the bike
swishes a fishtail
slams into the trunk
rider launched over
the car, down the road
hits hard on the asphalt

on his back, silent
raises slowly, a knee
again, and again
his buddy pulls over
stands by his friend

from the rear-crumpled car
climbs a young woman
stunned, laid plans
gone abruptly agley

from shops, stores

customers, staff
hearing the crash
drop what they're doing
pour lining the street
eyes drawn to the drama

a glance of an eye
scape of dreams
altered, forever.

The Ghost

She's beautiful, so
to give rise to desire
alluring, elegant
head held high
ears, tail erect
eyes lined black
lashes white as her coat.

Her ribs show stark
hip bones jut
the back of her spine
fur despoiled with oil
swollen teats sport milk
still suckling three pups.

She wanders wild
the ways of Cajón
appearing, to vanish
suddenly, silent
ghost of a wolf.
Chicken killer
neighbors grumble
surprised still alive
not yet been poisoned.

Offered a biscuit
the Ghost, guarded
slowly approaches
comes close, nibbles
rubs up my leg
lets me stroke her
the while snarling at males
sneaking up, sniffing
again she's in heat.

With dish full of kibble
I coax her down
the driveway, she eats
outside of the gate
soon braves the yard
before long, the house
coming now, often
dawn, noon, evening
her frame slowly fills out.

Bela suffers her, grudging
Capo growls and snarls
keeping his distance
Viva cat hates her
seeing a white devil
disappears for days
in her own time returning
but only when Ghost
is sure to be gone.

The months slip by
the Ghost, often
escaped from her compound
turns up for tidbits
kind word and touch
Bela still jealous
of shared attention
Capo, passed on.

Before the Ghost, Viva
would perch on my desk
beg to be brushed
curl up in my chair
whenever I left it
her presence, now scarce.

Capo: in memoriam

Crawling out of bushes
a coffee dog, colored
deep brown and black
accents of cream
short legs suited
for steep cafetal

I have the Sidekick
up by the main road
waiting at the drive
rough, rutted gravel
ladies need to be taxied
hen party at the house

box of biscuits in back
for just such occasion
hand out, speak softly
wary, the dog takes one
comes back for more
we're now cookie buddies

morning passes, he slips
back into the brush
later appears at the gate
Zooey barks him away
days passing, persevering
they finally become friends

Capo quickly learns
how to get what he wants
with nudge of his nose
sharp yap at the door
when Zooey passes on
Capo befriends Bela

idyllic, El Cajón
for a dog, trails, streets
rides to the store
Bela in back, Capo in front
nose in the wind
ears flapping breeze

with age outings dwindle
brief stints in the yard
spot of sun, soaking
settling on his bed
clouded eyes watch out
to raise alarm at trespass

one morning he doesn't rise
from rug in the shower
his shelter from storm
hours pass, he struggles
to breathe, as day ends
our Capo has gone.

The places he haunts
we expect still to see him
yet Capo keeps on
not being there
his ashes buried
where purple flowers bloom.

Note to my cousin

The note you wrote
some time ago telling
of five poems, sent off
to a poetry contest
bides in my mind.

I've read all your poems
— ones shared with me —
find infusing the verses
a vision distinctive
of place, of time
a mind quick, quirky, playful
genius not to be grasped
in a handful of short poems
out of all context.

A friend here, a writer
close, as a brother
sent one of his books
off seeking an agent
in response, nothing.
With stage roots in New York
and contacts in LA
he tries still to spark interest
in a screenplay, explaining
*Might as well give it
one last shot.*

For several years I labored
rendering a volume
of Spanish verse, admired
as poetry in English
working with the author
submitting the pages

to a university press
which consigned the manuscript
to their own editor
native tongue, not English
who so stepped on my lines
that I offered to purchase
the whole of the run
for promise to pulp
every last one.

Having passed now
three-quarters of a century
how droll to find ourselves
yearning for more
respect, recognition
all we've been gifted
not yet enough.

I'm not giving up
Paul said, having read
an early draft of this poem.
I'd enter more contests
was your retort
were I not so lazy.

Lines from a song
by Don Mclean sing
not only of Vincent —

This world was never meant for one
As beautiful as you.

Zazen

Viva the cat sits
spot of sun in the garden
time perfectly still

Rebecca

Break of day
let out the dog
shower, make coffee
a tractor rumbles
down the servidumbre
into the cafetal.

From Irina's childhood
best friend, her husband
and daughter, Rebecca
are coming for a stay
this afternoon, overnight
to leave the next day.

Rena, Hartmut
each rolling a suitcase
and, hefting a huge backpack
Rebecca, her strong frame
long and limber, sits lotus
as easy as chair.

Rebecca barely engages
in chat of elders
even so, it's clear
she's well schooled, sharp
English rescues her father
when he gropes for a word.

She teaches, elementary
in Herford, up and quit
in search of, something.
Anytime, I can find work
counters qualms of her parents
there's a big shortage.

Outside, after noon
eating, drinking, conversing
as the dusk darkens
up the road, grumbling
tractor pulling a wagon
packed with laborers, Nicas.

Men, women, children
day spent picking coffee
I wave a greeting
one girl, budding woman
hanging on, smiles
with free hand waves back.

Rebecca tells she made yoga friends
on a bus trip, before
I'm thinking, she says
to join them, Nicaragua
when my parents have left
Costa Rica, return home.

Our guests leave a note
raving views, colors, sounds
the beauty of this place
the hours shared
to not be forgotten.

Rebecca, the young girl
paths crossing, diverging
in these tropical woods
a moment, brief
very nearly unnoticed.

Monition

A dream, landscape
wanton destruction
in color, everything
black and white, silent
through eyes of a drone

from a pile of rubble
crawls an old woman
clutching her clothes
to keep herself cloaked
drone overhead hovers
the woman scrambles
desperate tries to escape

the drone stalks her
in terror the woman
throws up her arms
hugging her head
the drone zooms in
a burst of flame.

Fantasia

Top of the driveway
a bank-owned property
paved access to ours
cuts through the trees

house slowly rotting
a caretaker lived there
kept the place neat
the easement, too

day came the bank sold
real cheap, buyer said
thinking to flip it
make a quick profit

his efforts to fix up
most ill-conceived
each iteration
not proving improvement

he hauled in junkers
to be repaired, resold
or stripped for parts
hulks left to rust

he bought a white Husky
pure bred to impress girlfriend
who soon left, the dog
bore three mongrel pups

time passing, he skipped town
a neighbor lady now
and then comes to tidy
daily to feed the dogs

the drive, left unswept
of leaves shed from trees
of needles of pines
debris falls to my hands

orange plastic fingers
worn down to nubs
buy a new rake, thinking
save the good handle

rather, take the old rake
up the drive, lean it
at the gate to the yard
of the dwelling forsaken

days follow, the drive
seems to keep itself clean
of leaves, needles
other such detritus.

Dinner party with friends

Silence in the face of evil is itself evil:
God will not hold us guiltless.
Not to speak is to speak.
Not to act is to act.
— Dietrich Bonhoeffer

Twenty-sixteen we part ways
with those whose champion
bully Narcissus
other corner, his rival
really, no better
our circle of friends
shrinks much smaller.

Eight years having passed
an evening, at table
meal over, a guest
lips loosened by rum
with irony, speaks horror
genocide, a *nakba*
far away, Holy Land.

"*Time to go,*" some say
goodbyes as they leave
walk into the evening.

El Cajón, evening, on the veranda

Below, in the canyon
the stream, always there
hear the water, it flows

Watch, in the heavens
the moon wanes and waxes
neither lessens nor grows.

She

Viva shuns White Girl
comes at night, we're in bed
scratches at the screen door
asking in to be fed

again later wakes me
at my face, purring
nibbles my nose
licks at my lips

insisting I follow her
into the kitchen
top up her bowls
of kibble, of cream

or to the washroom
she waits at the basin
'til I crack the faucet
so she can sip

once more, to the door
to be escorted outside
before the white dog
shows up with the dawn.

Such disturbance of sleep
one might think annoying
but I find these moments
present time to ponder

being aroused
from deep in dreams
fantastical, magic
characters, scenes

dramas dissolving
even as eyes open
to this world, incanted
purported awake

and to this dream, my own
I remember beginning
She biting my lip bloody
leaving lasting impression.

Acknowledgments

She, Irina — my love, this dream, shared.

Made in the USA
Columbia, SC
01 November 2024

45314371R00054